JAPANESE SLANGUAGE

A **FUN** VISUAL GUIDE TO JAPANESE TERMS AND PHRASES BY MIKE ELLIS

GIBBS SMITH
TO ENRICH AND INSPIRE HUMANKIND

First Edition
14 13   5

Text © 2010 Mike Ellis
Illustrations © 2010 Rupert Bottenberg

Published by
Gibbs Smith
P.O. Box 667
Layton, Utah 84041

1.800.835.4993 orders
www.gibbs-smith.com

Design by Michel Vrana
Printed and bound in Hong Kong

Gibbs Smith books are printed on paper produced
from sustainable PEFC-certified forest/controlled
wood source.
Learn more at: www.pefc.org

Library of Congress Cataloging-in-Publication
Data

Ellis, Mike, 1961-
  Japanese slanguage : a fun visual guide to
Japanese terms and phrases /
Mike Ellis. — 1st ed.
      p. cm.
  Text in English and Japanese.
  ISBN-13: 978-1-4236-0748-9
  ISBN-10: 1-4236-0748-1
  1. Japanese language—Conversation and phrase
books—English. I. Title.
  PL539.E54 2010
  495.6'83421—dc22
                                        2009053857

CONTENTS

United Way

United Way
of San Diego County

HOW TO USE THIS BOOK

If you want to learn the basics of Japanese but traditional methods seem overwhelming or intimidating, this book is for you! Just follow the directions below and soon you'll be able to say dozens of words and phrases in Japanese.

• Follow the illustrated prompts to say the phrase quickly and smoothly. If all the words or syllables are in black, say them with equal emphasis on each one. If a word or syllable is in red, put the emphasis on that word or syllable. While your pronunciation may not be exact, you'll be able to be understood if you speak clearly and evenly.

• Learn to string together words or phrases to create many more phrases.

• Draw your own pictures to help with memorization and pronunciation.

Note: This product may produce Americanized Japanese.

For free sound bytes, visit slanguage.com.

GREETINGS AND RESPONSES

Hello
こんにちは　*Konnichiha*

Cone Knee Chee Wah

Good-bye
さようなら　*Sayounara*

Sigh Oh Notta

Good evening
こんばんは　*Konbanha*

Cone Bun Wah

Excuse me
すみません　*Sumimasen*

Sue Me Mustn't

Good morning
おはよう！ *Ohayou!*

Ohio

Gladly
喜んで　*Yorokonde*

Yodo Cone Day

To your health
お大事に　*ODaijiNi*

Oh Die Jeanie

Welcome
ようこそ！ *Youkoso!*

Yoko So

Okay
オーケー　*O ke*

Okay

You're welcome
どういたしまして
Douitashimashite

Don't Touch My Moustache

Congratulations
おめでとう　*Omedetou*

Oh May Day Toe

What's the weather like?
どんな天気ですか？
DonnaTenkiDesuka?

Don Not Ten Key Desk ah?

MONEY AND SHOPPING

A store
店 *Mise*

Me Say

A bank
銀行 *Ginkou*

Ginko

Department store
デパート *Depaato*

Day Pa Toe

Purchase
購入 *Kounyuu*

Cone You

To buy
買う *Kau*

Cow

To get in line
並ぶ *Narabu*

Notta Boo

Small item
小物 *Komono*

Comb Oh No

Clothing
服 *Fuku*

Who Coo

Hat
帽子　*Boushi*

Stain
染み　*Shimi*

Jewel
宝石　*Houseki*

Skirt
スカート　*Sukato*

Bow She

She Me

Hoe Say Key

Scott Oh

Coat
コート *Koto*

Coat Oh

Pants
ズボン *Zubon*

Zoo Bone

Pajamas
パジャマ *Pajama*

Pajama

Sleeve
袖 *Sode*

So Day

ENTERTAINMENT AND SPORTS

Cinema
シネマ   *Shinema*

She Nay Ma

Piano
ピアノ   *Piano*

Piano

Saxophone
サクソフォーン   *Sakusofon*

Sock So Phone

A park
公園   *Kouen*

Cohen

Choir
聖歌隊　*SeikaTai*

Poem
詩　*Shi*

Theatrical
芝居の　*ShibaiNo*

A sound
音　*Oto*

Sake a Tie

She

She Buy No

Oh Toe

A painting
絵　*E*

Eh

Picnic
ピクニック　*Pikunikku*

Pea Coup Knee Coup

Portrait
肖像　*Shouzou*

Shows Oh

A comedy
コメディ　*Komedi*

Comb May Dee

Gymnastics
体操　*Taisou*

Tie Sew

Cards
カード　*Kaado*

Cod Oh

Game
ゲーム　*Geemu*

Gay Moo

Tennis
テニス　*Tenisu*

Ten Knee Sue

Kite
凧 *Tako*

Taco

Skate
スケート *Sukeeto*

Sue Kay Toe

Upset
動揺 *Douyou*

Do Yo

Disappointment
失望 *Shitsubou*

Sheet Sue Bow

Woman
女 *Onna*

On Nah

Man
男 *Otoko*

Oh Taco

Friend
友人 *Yuujin*

You Jean

Last name
苗字 *Myouji*

Me Oh Gee

First name
名前 *Namae*

Nam Eye

Girl
少女 *Shoujo*

Show Joe

Boy
少年 *Shounen*

Show Nen

Baby
赤ちゃん *Akachan*

Akka Chen

Crowd
群衆 *Gunshuu*

Goon Shoe

Mother
母 *Haha*

Ha Ha

Father
父 *Chichi*

Chi Chi

Daughter
娘 *Musume*

Moo Sue May

Son
息子 *Musuko*

Brother
兄弟 *Kyoudai*

Sister
姉妹 *Shimai*

Grandmother
祖母 *Sobo*

Moo Sue Ko

Key Yo Die

She My

So Bow

Grandfather
祖父 *Sofu*

Sew Foo

Husband
夫 *Otto*

Oh Toe

Wife
妻 *Tsuma*

Sue Ma

Granddaughter
孫娘 *MagoMusume*

Ma Go Moo Sue May

Grandson
孫息子　*MagoMusuko*

Ma Go Moose Ko

Girlfriend
彼女　*Kanojo*

Con Oh Joe

Boyfriend
彼氏　*Kareshi*

Cod Eshy

To reside
住む *Sumu*

Sue Moo

To have fun
楽しむ *Tanoshimu*

Ton Know She Moo

To smell
匂う *Niou*

Knee Yo

To dress
装う *Yosoou*

Yo So

To read
読む *Yomu*

Yo Moo

To hope
望む *Nozomu*

Nose Oh Moo

To meet
会う *Au*

Ow

To sink
沈む *Shizumu*

She Zoo Moo

Eye Sue

To love
愛す *Aisu*

Oh Sue

To push
押す *Osu*

Here
ここ *Koko*

Cocoa

Really
本当に *Hontouni*

Hone Tony

How
どう *Dou*

Doe

More
もっと *Motto*

Moe Toe

Almost
ほとんど   *Hotondo*

Hoe Tone Doe

In the middle / At the center
中央で   *ChuuouDe*

Chew Owe Day

Sometimes
時々   *Tokidoki*

Toe Key Doe Key

Always
いつも   *Itsumo*

Eat Sue Moe

At first
最初に *Saishoni*

Sigh Show Knee

Finally
最終的に *Saishuutekini*

Sigh Shoe Tech Key Knee

Already
既に *Sudeni*

Sue Day Knee

Recently
最近 *Saikin*

Sigh Keen

Fortunately
幸い *Saiwai*

Sigh Why

Slowly
ゆっくり *Yukkuri*

You Cootie

Seriously
真剣に *Shinkenni*

Sheen Ken Knee

Properly
適切に *Tekisetsuni*

Take Key Set Sue Knee

Nowhere/Anywhere
どこにも *Dokonimo*

Doe Coney Moe

Silently
静かに *Shizukani*

She Zoo Connie

Inside
内部 *Naibu*

Nye Boo

Outside
外部 *Gaibu*

Guy Boo

Great, charming
素敵 *Suteki*

Sue Techy

Handsome
ハンサム *hansamu*

Han Summer

Big
大きい *Ookii*

Oh Key

Fat
脂肪 *Shibou*

She Bow

Blonde
金髪　*Kinpatsu*

Keen Pot Sue

Hardworking
勤勉　*Kinben*

Keen Ben

Clever
利口　*Rikou*

Rick Oh

Outgoing
外向的　*Gaikouteki*

Guy Coat Techy

Generous
寛大　*Kandai*

Con Die

Intelligent
知的　*Chiteki*

Cheat Techy

Disappointed
失望　*Shitsubou*

Sheet Sue Bow

Popular
ポピュラー　*Popyuraa*

Pope You'd A

Clumsy
不器用　*Bukiyou*

Boo Key Yo

Honest
正直　*Shoujiki*

Show Jee Key

Kind
親切　*Shinsetsu*

Sheen Set Sue

Free
自由　*Jiyuu*

Jee You

Last
最終 *Saishuu*

Sigh Shoe

Likewise
同様に *Douyouni*

Doe Yo Knee

Rough
荒い *Arai*

Odd Eye

Hard
固い *Katai*

Cot Tie

Pointed
とがった   *Togatta*

Toe Gotta

Blunt
鈍い   *Nibui*

Knee Buoy

Fast
速い   *Hayai*

Hi Eye

Dangerous
危険   *Kiken*

Key Ken

PRONOUNS, CONJUNCTIONS, AND PREPOSITIONS

She
彼女 *Kanojo*

Con Oh Joe

He
彼 *Kare*

Cod Eh

If
もし *Moshi*

Moe She

Near
近い *Chikai*

Cheek Eye

Beside
のとなり　*Notonari*

No Toe Knotty

While, during
ちゅう　*Chuu*

Chew

Without
せずに　*Sezuni*

Say Zoo Knee

When
いつ　*Itsu*

Eat Sue

How
どのように   *Donoyouni*

Doe No Yo Knee

Outside of
の外   *Nosoto*

No So Toe

So
そのように   *Sonoyouni*

So No Yo Knee

Telephone
電話　*Denwa*

Den Wah

Stove
ストーブ　*Sutoubu*

Stow Boo

Bed
ベッド　*Beddo*

Bed Doe

Sofa
ソファー　*Sofa*

Sofa

Bench
ベンチ *Benchi*

Benchy

Carpet
カーペット *Kaapetto*

Cop Pet Toe

Sheet
シート *Shiito*

She Toe

Trash
ごみ *Gomi*

Go Me

Video
ビデオ *Bideo*

Bee Day Oh

Bedroom
寝室 *Shinshitsu*

Sheen Sheet Sue

Garage
ガレージ *gareeji*

Gutter Age

Curtain
カーテン *Kaaten*

Cotton

Key, lock
鍵　*Kagi*

Vacuum cleaner
掃除機　*Soujiki*

Corgi

So Jee Key

OFFICE AND PROFESSIONS

Calculator
計算機 *Keisanki*

Kay Sun Key

Book
本 *Hon*

Hone

Office
オフィス *Ofisu*

Oh Fee Sue

Boss
ボス *Bosu*

Bow Sue

Appointment
アポイントメント
Apointomento

A Point Toe Meant Toe

Actor
俳優　*Haiyuu*

Hi You

Teacher
教師　*Kyoushi*

Key Oh She

Lawyer
弁護士　*Bengoshi*

Ben Go She

Doctor
医師 *Ishi*

Pilot
パイロット *Pairotto*

Mechanic
整備士 *Seibishi*

Hairstylist
美容師 *Biyoushi*

E She

Pie'd Oh Toe

Say Bee She

Bee Oh She

Fireman
消防士 *Shouboushi*

Librarian
司書 *Shisho*

Soldier
兵士 *Heishi*

Show Bow She

She Show

Hey She

Cigarette
タバコ *Tabako*

Tobacco

Joe's Eye

Pill
錠剤 *Jouzai*

Fever
熱 *Netsu*

Net Sue

Runny nose
鼻水 *Hanamizu*

Hana Me Zoo

Weak
弱い *Yowai*

Yo Eye

Doctor
医師 *Ishi*

E She

Sponge
スポンジ *Suponji*

Spongy

Breathing
呼吸 *Kokyuu*

Coke You

Heart
心臓　*Shinzou*

Bandage
包帯　*Houtai*

Disease
病気　*Byouki*

Life
人生　*Jinsei*

Sheens Oh

Hoe Tie

Bee Owe Key

Jean Say

To die
死ぬ *Shinu*

Eye
目 *Me*

Tooth
歯 *Hu*

Stomach
胃 *I*

She Knew

May

Ha

E

Throat
のど *Nodo*

No Doe

Ear
耳 *Mimi*

Me Me

Cow

Face
顔 *Kao*

Finger
指 *Yubi*

You Bee

Brow
まゆ *Mayu*

My You

Elbow
肘　*Hiji*

He Jee

Navel
へそ　*Heso*

Hay So

Forehead
額　*Hitai*

He Tie

POLITICS AND LAW ENFORCEMENT

Gunshot
銃撃　*Juugeki*

Jew Gay Key

Weapon
兵器　*Heiki*

Hey Key

To fight
戦う　*Tatakau*

Tata Cow

Civilian
民間人　*Minkanjin*

Mean Con Jean

Military
軍　*Gun*

Goon

Leader
リーダー　*Riidaa*

Reed Ah

Student
生徒　*Seito*

Say Toe

Notebook
ノート　*Nouto*

Know Toe

Sheet
シート　*Shiito*

She Toe

Keyboard
キーボード　*Kibodo*

Key Bow Doe

Exam
試験　*Shiken*

Word
単語　*Tango*

Pen
ペン　*Pen*

High school
高校　*Koukou*

She Ken

Tongue Go

Pen

Cocoa

One
一 *Ichi*

Eachy

Knee

Two
二 *Ni*

Three
三 *San*

Sun

She

Four
四 *Shi*

Five 五 *Go*	**Go**
Six 六 *Roku*	**Rock**
Seven 七 *Shichi*	**She Chee**
Eight 八 *Hachi*	**Hutchy**

Nine 九 *Kyuu*	**Cue**
Ten 十 *Juu*	**Jew**
Sunday 日曜日 *Nichiyoubi*	**Knee Chee Yo Bee**
Monday 月曜日 *Getsuyoubi*	**Gets Yo Bee**

Tuesday
火曜日 *Kayoubi*

Key Yo Bee

Wednesday
水曜日 *Suiyoubi*

Swee Yo Bee

Thursday
木曜日 *Mokuyoubi*

Moe Coo Yo Bee

Friday
金曜日 *Kinyoubi*

Keen Yo Bee

Saturday
土曜日　*Doyoubi*

Yesterday
昨日　*Kinou*

Day before yesterday
おととい　*Ototoi*

At that time
その時　*Sonotoki*

Doe Yo Bee

Key No

Oh Toe Toy

So No Toe Key

Noon
正午 *Shougo*

Show Go

Afternoon
午後 *Gogo*

Go Go

Recently
最近 *Saikin*

Sigh Keen

The future
未来 *Mirai*

Meade Eye

Fall
秋 *Aki*

A Key

Spring
春 *Haru*

Hod U

Summer
夏 *Natsu*

Not Sue

Winter
冬 *Fuyu*

Foo You

City
都市 *Toshi*

Toe She

Street
通り *Toori*

Toady

Store
店 *Mise*

Me Say

Prison
刑務所 *Keimusho*

Kay Moo Show

Bookstore
書店　*Shoten*

Shot Ten

Tower
塔　*Tou*

Toe

Office
オフィス　*Ofisu*

Oh Fee Sue

Fire station
消防署　*Shoubousho*

Show Bow Show

Sail
帆　*Ho*

Hoe

Cart
カート　*Kaato*

Cot Toe

Sidewalk
歩道　*Hodou*

Hoe Doe

Traffic light
信号　*Shingou*

Sheen Go

Stop sign
ストップサイン
Sutoppusain

Sue Toe Poo Sign

A turn
回転　*Kaiten*

Kite Ten

Jet
ジェット　*Jietto*

Jet Toe

Port
港　*Minato*

Me Not Toe

A bank
銀行 *Ginkou*

Ginko

Airport
空港 *Kuukou*

Kook Oh

Taxi
タクシー *Takushi*

Tock She

Bus
バス *Basu*

Bus Sue

Car
車　*Kuruma*

Coo'd U Ma

Train
列車　*Ressha*

Ray Shah

Ticket
チケット　*Chiketto*

Cheek Ket Toe

Restaurant
レストラン　*Resutoran*

Rest Toad On

Hotel
ホテル *Hoteru*

Hot Tade Ooh

Toy Ray

Restroom
トイレ *Toire*

Shoe

State
州 *Shuu*

Say Boo

Western
西部 *Seibu*

Eastern
東部 *Toubu*

Border
国境 *Kokkyou*

Toe Boo
Coke Yo

FOOD AND RESTAURANTS

. . . I'd like
をください   *Okudasai*

Oh Cuda Sigh

(This phrase goes on the end of words or phrases to express asking for something, for example, "Me Zoo Oh Cuda Sigh" means "Water, I'd like.")

To drink
飲む   *Nomu*

No Moo

To eat
食べる   *TabeRu*

Top Bade U

Beef
牛肉 *Gyuuniku*

Gee You Knee Coo

Meat
肉 *Niku*

Knee Coo

No meat
肉なし *Niku nashi*

Knee Coo Nosh

A vegetable
野菜 *Yasai*

Ya Sigh

A drink
飲み物   *Nomimono*

No Me Moan Oh

Water
水   *Mizu*

Me Zoo

Wine
ワイン   *Wain*

Wine

Potato
じゃがいも   *Jagaimo*

Jog Eye Moe

Rice
米 *Kome*

Comb May

Mustard
マスタード *Masutaado*

Muss Todd Oh

Toast
トースト *Tosuto*

Toast Oh

Cake
ケーキ *Keiki*

Kay Key

Pie
パイ *Pai*

Sausage
ソーセージ *Soseiji*

Cocoa
ココア *Kokoa*

Spoon
スプーン *Supun*

Pie

So Say Jee

Cocoa Ah

Spoon

Knife
ナイフ　*Naifu*

Nye Foo

Fork
フォーク　*Fooku*

Foo Coo

Plate
プレート　*Pureteo*

Poo'd Ate Toe

Cup
カップ　*Kappu*

Cop Poo

Salt
塩　*Shio*

She Oh

Spicy
スパイシー　*Supaishi*

Spy She

Menu
メニュー　*Menyu*

Menu

Delicious
美味しい　*Oishii*

Oh E She